APR - 2012

Grow Your Own

Potatoes

Helen Lanz

SEA-TO-SEA

Mankato Collingwood London

To Mark, because your head reminds me of a potato

This edition first published in 2012 by
Sea-to-Sea Publications
Distributed by Black Rabbit Books
P.O. Box 3263, Mankato, Minnesota 56002

Copyright © Sea-to-Sea Publications 2012

Printed in China

9 8 7 6 5 4 3 2

Published by arrangement with the Watts Publishing Group Ltd, London.

Library of Congress Cataloging-in-Publication Data

Lanz, Helen.
 Potatoes / by Helen Lanz.
     p. cm. -- (Grow your own)
 Includes index.
 ISBN 978-1-59771-312-2 (library binding)
 1. Potatoes--Juvenile literature. 2. Vegetable gardening--Juvenile literature. I. Title.
 SB211.P8L37 2012
 635'.21--dc22
                         2011001220
Series editor: Sarah Peutrill
Art director: Jonathan Hair
Design: Jane Hawkins
Photography: Victoria Coombs/Ecoscene (unless otherwise credited)

Credits: Tomas Bercic/istockphoto: 12b. Courtesy of Crown © FERA /SPL: 20b. Richard Goerg/istockphoto: 9bl. Joe Gough/
istockphoto: 6c. GFDL/CC 2.5: 20m. Marjanneke de Jong/Shutterstock: 25b. Kativ/istockphoto: 21br. Helen Lanz: 10t, 19t, 23.
Monkey Business/Shutterstock: 26t. Moodboard/Corbis: front cover b. Dan Moore/istockphoto: 1, 31. Penny Oakley: 7m, 15t,
15b, 16m and 18b. Vibeke Olsen/istockphoto: 20t. Quanthem/istockphoto: 6b. Dr Marlin E Rice/AgstockUSA/SPL: 21tr. Steve
Snyder/istockphoto: 21bl. Liz Van Steenburgh/Shutterstock: 27b. Sally Wallis/Shutterstock: front cover t.
Every attempt has been made to clear copyright. Should there be any inadvertent omission please apply to the
publisher for rectification.

Thanks to Jasmine Clarke and Tony Field, seasoned gardeners, for kindly sharing their gardening knowledge.
The author and publisher would like to thank the models who took part in this book.

February 2011
RD/6000006415/001

Safety Notice:

Gardening is fun! There are a few basic rules you must follow, however. Always garden with an adult; any pesticides and fertilizers should be handled by adults only and applied to specified plants only; wear appropriate clothing and footwear and always wash your hands when you have finished in the garden.

Contents

Words in **bold** are in the glossary on page 29.

Why Grow Your Own Potatoes?

Do you like to eat sausages with mashed potatoes, or how about french fries? Most of us like to *eat* potatoes in one form or another. But have you ever thought about *growing* them?

▲ Potatoes can be prepared in all sorts of ways: mashed, baked, fried, boiled, chipped, or roasted. What's your favorite way?

Fresh Flavor

You will never cut through a fresher, crispier potato than one you've just pulled up from your garden. Often, fruit and vegetables that you have grown yourself have real flavor, partly because you can eat them just as soon as they have been picked.

◀ Potatoes that you cook straight from the garden are hard, crisp, and dense.

Room to Grow

You don't need much room to grow your own potatoes, either. Did you know that you can grow them in a growbag or pot if you don't have a vegetable plot?

But one of the best things about growing your own potatoes is that it's fun!

▲ You can grow potatoes in small places—even in buckets and bags!

Flower

Leaf

Stem

Root

Young tuber

Old seed potato

SCIENCE SPOT *What Is a Tuber?*
The potato is a stem tuber. A tuber is a **bulbous** growth that grows on the stem or root of a plant. The bulbous stem tuber stores food, or **nutrients**, for the plant but it can also be dug up and eaten—this is the actual potato.

Be Prepared!

So, you've decided to grow your own! It's a good idea to think about what you will need before you get going.

Think Ahead

You will be outside a lot digging around in dirt so you will need some old clothes that your parents or carers won't mind if you get dirty. And for your feet, a pair of rubber boots or old sneakers will do the job.

You also need to decide where you will be planting your potatoes—in a pot, growbag, or in the ground.

▶ If you are planting in a pot or growbag, you will need some potting mix.

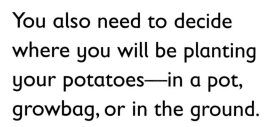

8

What Else Do I Need?

You may decide to use gardening gloves, but these aren't necessary. A fork and trowel may be useful.

You will definitely need some **seed potatoes** (you can buy a bag of these from a garden center). An egg carton is useful at the start to **presprout** your potatoes (see pages 12–13).

Finally, you will need a watering can and some plant food to help your potatoes grow.

Top Tip!

It's a good idea to keep a growing diary, writing down everything, from the potato type to how and when you did things. This will help if you decide to do it again, and will be fun to look back on. If you have a camera, taking photos as you go along would also be a good idea.

Choose Your Variety

There are a lot of potato **varieties** to choose from.

▲ *Rocket potatoes are good for boiling.*

Early Potatoes

Early potatoes can be planted early in the growing season (see page 28), but after the main **frosts**, and should be ready to **harvest** about 10 weeks later. Many early potatoes avoid a lot of the problems that sometimes affect potatoes, such as **blight** (see page 20). Varieties of early potato include Onaway and Yukon Gold.

Midseason Potatoes

Plant midseason potatoes and salad varieties at the beginning of the growing season, but just after first early potatoes. These will usually take about 13 weeks before they are ready to harvest. Second early varieties include: Frontier Russet, Estima, Kestrel, and Maris Peer. Salad, or new, potatoes include Fingerlings, named after their shape.

Estima   Kestrel

▲ *Estima is a popular variety to grow. It is good for mashing, boiling, and baking. Kestrel potatoes are good for making fries and roasting.*

Late Potatoes

These can be planted in the middle of the growing season. They take about 20 weeks before they are ready to harvest. Late potato varieties can get more **diseases** and **pests** (see Top Tip below and pages 20–21), so it is worth checking which varieties survive such problems the best. Maris Piper, King Edward, and Melody are late potatoes.

▶ These are Desiree potatoes, a late potato variety.

Maris Piper

Melody

▲ Maris Piper is a good, all-around cooking variety. Melody potatoes don't often get diseases.

Top Tip!

Check the seed potato bag to see exactly when you should plant your chosen variety, what diseases that particular variety generally avoids, and how best to cook it. You can also check the Internet or ask at your local garden center for more information.

Presprout the Tuber

Eye

Potatoes grow from seed potatoes, rather than seeds. These are older potatoes that have been stored, and start to **sprout** "eyes." You need to encourage your seed potatoes to sprout a bit more before planting. This is called presprouting.

▲ *The eyes are the buds that grow into the new potato plants.*

Free From Disease

It is a good idea to buy seed potatoes from a garden center, rather than just use old potatoes from your cupboard that have started to sprout. These may carry a disease that the original potato had. This will be passed on to any potatoes that grow from the old potato.

▶ *Properly grown seed potatoes are unlikely to carry diseases.*

Step-by-Step

1. Before the start of the growing season (see page 28), prepare your seed potatoes. Check the bag to see when you should plant your variety of potato. Presprout them about four or so weeks before planting.

2. To start your seed potatoes, choose a number of healthy-looking potatoes that have started to sprout.

3. Place each seed potato in the bottom of an egg carton, one potato in each cup, with the eyes upward.

4. Put the egg carton on a bright windowsill, but not in direct sunlight. Leave to sprout for four weeks or so.

Top Tip!

As your potatoes sprout, the sprouts should be green, not white. If they are white, they are not getting enough light so move them to a new spot.

Pot or Plot?

▲ *Potatoes prefer slightly acidic soil, but will grow in any soil (see pages 24–25).*

To help keep your trench straight, you can use string tied to two pieces of wood at either end of your trench. ▼

While your seed potatoes are presprouting, you can prepare your pot or plot.

The Best Place

Potatoes love warm and sunny spots, with plenty of direct sunlight and no shade—they don't like the frost at all. They also like **well-drained soil**.

Preparing the Plot

To grow your potatoes in the ground, you must prepare the soil well. Dig in plenty of **compost**. Do this well ahead of time and keep working the soil over.

Dig your **trench** about 5 inches (12 cm) deep. If you have more than one row, make sure the rows are about 24 inches (60 cm) apart.

Top Tip!

Potatoes do need a good depth (height) of soil to grow in, but early varieties don't need too much room.

Preparing the Pot (or Growbag!)

Early potatoes will also grow well in a large container or even a sturdy plastic bag. You will need to make sure there are holes in the bottom to allow the water to drain out.

Then put gravel and large stones into the bottom of your container or bag to help with **drainage**.

Add a mixture of potting mix and compost until it is at least 5 inches (12 cm) deep.

Top Tip!

The pot or bag will get very heavy when you put the soil in, so position it where you want it before you fill it with soil.

15

Sowing the Seed Potato

When the sprouts on the seed potatoes are between about ¾ inch (1.5 cm long)—four or so weeks after presprouting—your seed potatoes are ready to plant outside.

Step-by-Step

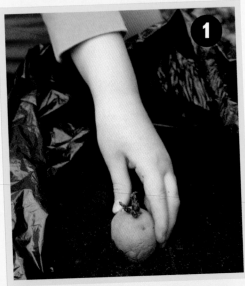

1. Make sure you place the seed potato in the soil with the sprouts pointing upward.

2. In the vegetable plot, plant your seed potatoes about 12 inches (30 cm) away from each other.

SCIENCE SPOT — *What It Takes to Grow*

Most plants start out as seeds (or in a potato's case, a seed potato). To grow, or **germinate**, seeds need dark, damp, and warm conditions—soil is the perfect place. The roots develop first; these take up water and nutrients from the soil, which are then moved all around the plant through its veins.

3. For potatoes in pots, leave about 6 inches (15 cm) between each potato and some space between the potato and the side of the bag or pot. Place the first seed potato in the middle of the bag and arrange the others around it.

4. Cover the potatoes with about 3 inches (7.5 cm) of soil. Do not damage the shoots. In a vegetable plot, use the soil that has come out of the trench to cover your seed potatoes.

Top Tip!
If you use a large plant pot, about 10 inches (25 cm) across, plant two or three seed potatoes.

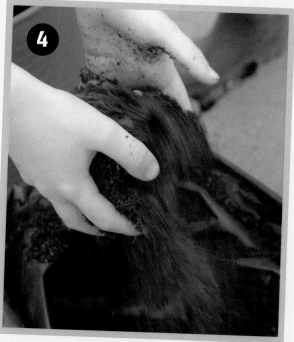

Tending the Crop

As soon as you have planted your seed potatoes, water them well.

Water Well

Check your potatoes regularly to see if they need a drink, especially in hot weather. However, make sure the soil does not become **waterlogged**. To see if you need to water, poke your finger into the soil. If it is damp, you may not need to water just yet.

▲ Some watering cans have special spray heads but you don't have to use one of these.

◄ Soil may look dry on the top, but be damp underneath.

Hilling

Two weeks after the first green shoots appear, you will need to cover the plants up again! This is called "hilling." Because potatoes are stem tubers, they grow on the stem of the plant. As the plant grows taller, the potatoes therefore emerge above the soil. However, too much light turns the tuber green. To stop them from going green, cover the plant with soil every two to three weeks.

◄ *It is not safe to eat green potatoes. They will give you a stomachache.*

▲ *The first green shoots will begin to appear after about two weeks.*

◄ *It seems odd to cover the plants with soil, but be sure to leave the tops of the plants showing through. Throw away any green potatoes.*

Green potatoes

Feed Them!

Ask your grown-up helper to add liquid feed to your plants in containers about a month after planting them.

PLANT FOOD

500ml ℮

Pest Patrol!

Checking your potatoes regularly is the best way to keep them healthy. If you do notice any problems, you can deal with them quickly.

Blight

This is one of the worst diseases that potatoes can get. It affects the leaves first and eventually can affect the whole plant, including the growing potatoes themselves.

◀ If you notice brown patches like this, your plant has blight. It is best to remove the infected plant and throw it away.

Common Scab

This disease affects the skin of the potato. It can help to dig in lots of **manure** before you plant your seed potatoes, because potatoes in dry or light soil seem to get it the most.

▼ This potato has scab—raised patches that can split the surface.

Colorado Potato Beetle!

Check the underside of leaves for the orange egg clumps of the Colorado potato beetles. If you see any, destroy them. Both the adults (yellowish bugs with black stripes), and the larvae (dark red or orange with black spots) eat potato foliage.

Slugs and Wireworms

Wireworms are the larvae of the click beetle. They tunnel into the growing potatoes and ruin them. Digging the earth well before planting helps protect against wireworm. Remove any that you find as you dig.

▲ Wireworms make holes in potatoes.

Sorting out Slugs

If you do have trouble with slugs, you could try to combat them by encouraging frogs to come into your yard to eat them! Or you can pick slugs off your crops.

▲ A pond or shallow container of water may attract frogs, the gardener's best friend!

▲ Hungry slugs like to snack on potatoes.

Harvest

Having looked after your crop well, it won't be long before it's time for harvest.

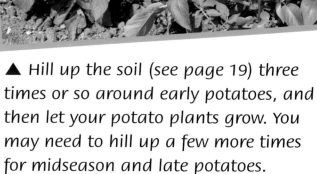

▲ Hill up the soil (see page 19) three times or so around early potatoes, and then let your potato plants grow. You may need to hill up a few more times for midseason and late potatoes.

How Long?

If you have planted an early potato variety, your potato crop should be ready about 10 weeks after planting. If you have planted a midseason variety or late potato, these will take a little longer to grow (see page 28). You can tell when your crop is ready because the plants will often flower. When the plant flowers, check to see if there are potatoes.

If you find some and they are the size of hen's eggs, they're ready, so dig deep! It's just like looking for buried treasure!

Enjoy your prize!

Top Tip!

Only take the number of potatoes you need. Leave the others in the ground to continue growing. If you do store picked potatoes, keep them in cloth or paper sacks in a dark, dry place.

What Kind of Soil?

Potatoes grow happily in different types of soil. They do prefer slightly acidic soil, but will grow in any.

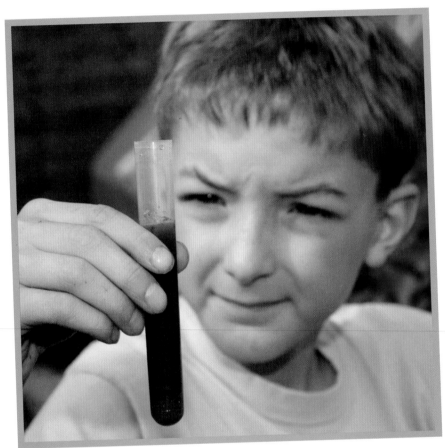

How Acidic?

Soil can be neutral (pH of 7), acid (pH below 7), or alkaline (pH above 7). You can test your soil to see what pH it is. You can buy a kit from your local garden center.

◄ *Soil-testing kits are quick and easy to use.*

Different Types of Soil

There are also different types of soil. The main types are sandy, silty, or clay. Soil may vary in different places even around your vegetable patch.

◄ *This soil is mostly clay.*

Do a hand test to see what yours is:

sandy—feels gritty to touch; won't hold together as a ball; warms up quickly, so helps plants' growth, but dries out quickly

silty—feels smooth; will roll but not hold together as a ball; is best soil type for growing most plants

clay—feels sticky; can roll it into a ball; retains moisture well

It is possible to have a combination of these.

▶ *Sandy soil will run through your fingers easily.*

Top Tip!

When you know your soil type, you can choose potato plants that suit your soil the best. Check online, on the seed pack, or ask at your local garden center. You can also add things, such as fertilizers and compost, to your soil to change its pH.

▼ *Digging in compost makes your soil less alkaline and better for growing potatoes.*

Perfect Potatoes

▲ *Don't forget to eat the skin! Many of the vitamins are stored here.*

Potatoes are a tasty food that can be enjoyed in many ways. They are good for you, too! Potatoes are very **nutritious**. They contain **vitamins** B, B_6, and C, as well as the important **mineral**, potassium.

Preparing Your Potatoes

Before you get creative with you potatoes, you need to wash them well in cold water. You may need a potato brush for stubborn dirt.

Potato Recipes

Potatoes cannot be eaten raw, but there are many ways to cook them. You can boil, bake, roast, or fry them. Baking is one of the healthiest ways to cook potatoes because there is so much **fiber** in the skin. Many recipes include potatoes, from scalloped potatoes to soups and stews. Why not try the recipe opposite, or search the Internet for more ideas?

Make a Potato Crusted Pizza

Ingredients
- 14 oz. (400 g) large russet Idaho potatoes, peeled
- 1½ cups (175 g) self-rising flour
- 1 tsp baking powder
- 2 tsp mixed dried herbs
- ¾ cup (150 ml) milk

Topping:
- 2 cups (150 g) broccoli florets
- 2 tbsp tomato paste
- 2 tomatoes and 1 pepper
- ½ cup (50 g) cheese, grated

With Your Grownup Helper:

1. Cut the potatoes into small pieces and boil in water for 10 minutes. Steam the broccoli for a few minutes then put to one side. Drain the potatoes well and allow to cool, then mash.

2. Sift the flour and baking powder into a bowl. Stir in the potato and herbs. Add the milk and mix to form a soft dough. Pour onto a floured surface and knead lightly to form a smooth ball.

4. Place the ball onto a greased cookie sheet. Press it out evenly into a 9 inch (23 cm) circle. Put into the oven at 425°F (220°C) and bake for 10 minutes.

5. Remove the base and lower the oven temperature to 400°F (200°C).

6. Spread the tomato paste over the base; slice the tomato and pepper and arrange on top, then scatter the broccoli and cheese on.

7. Bake in the oven for a further 8–10 minutes until the cheese has melted and the edge of the base is crisp.

Growing Calendar

Here's an "at-a-glance" guide to the growing year. Planting and growing times vary, depending on where you live.

Early Winter (Dec–Jan)

Plan your crop. Choose your potato varieties.

Late Winter (Jan–Feb)

Presprout first early seed potatoes for four weeks at the end of this period.

Early Spring (March–April)

Dig over your plot, adding compost or manure. Plant first early varieties at the beginning of this period.

Presprout midseason seed potatoes for four weeks at the beginning of this period. Presprout late season potatoes for four weeks in the middle of this period.

Water, feed, and hill first earlies. Cover potatoes if weather is frosty.

Late Spring (April–May)

Plant midseason varieties at the beginning of this period. Plant late season crop potatoes in the middle of this period.

Keep checking, watering, hilling, and feeding your early and midseason and late season potatoes.

Early Summer (June–July)

Keep checking, watering, hilling, and feeding your midseason potatoes.

First early potatoes will be ready for harvesting.

Late Summer (July–Aug)

Keep checking, watering, hilling, and feeding your late season potatoes.

Midseason potatoes will be ready for harvesting.

Early Fall (Sept–Oct)

Late season potatoes will be ready for harvesting.

Late Fall (Oct–Nov)

Dig over your plot, adding compost or manure ready for next year's crop.

Gardening Glossary

blight: a disease that is especially bad for potatoes.

bulbous: something that is a big, bulging shape.

compost: a mixture of soil and rotted plants used to improve soil in the ground before planting, and to fertilize plants to help them grow.

disease: an illness.

drainage: in this case, to allow water to flow through the soil and leave the plant pot or growbag, so the plant's roots don't rot.

fiber: the roughage in food, such as the skin of fruit or a potato.

frost: frozen water droplets that freeze on the ground.

germinate: the point when a root and leaf break through a seed case and the seed begins to grow.

harvest: the gathering in of crops, in this case, vegetables.

manure: fertilizer, waste from animals such as horses and pigs.

minerals: natural substances that are in food that are good for your body and health.

nutrients: something that gives goodness needed for growing or being healthy.

nutritious: something that is healthy for you to eat.

pests: insects or animals that are destructive to a plant, such as slugs or greenfly.

presprout: to encourage seed potatoes to sprout before planting.

root: the part of a plant below the ground that takes the nutrients, or goodness, from the soil to the rest of the plant.

seed potatoes: the tuber that is used to grow new potato plants.

sprout: to produce new growth such as the "eyes" of a potato.

trench: a small ditch in the soil to plant the seed potatoes in.

varieties: types of a plant.

vitamins: natural substances that are in food that are good for your body and health.

waterlogged: over-watered, or wet.

well-drained soil: soil that allows water to seep out of it, so that the soil doesn't get too wet and soggy.

Index

Useful Web Sites

www.kidsgardening.org/
The National Gardening Association believes that when you garden you grow. Their comprehensive gardening resource web site for children is highly inspirational.

http://home.howstuffworks.com/ potatoes1.htm
Information about growing your own potatoes, with handy tips and recipes.

http://www.wisconsinpotatoes.com/ AboutPotatoes/FunFacts.html
Find out all you need to know, and more, about potatoes, including some fun facts!

Gardening Club

Have you enjoyed growing your own? How about joining a gardening club? Your school may have one. You could grow fruit and vegetables or make ladybug homes to help attract them to your garden. If your school doesn't have a gardening club, why not talk to your teacher about setting one up?

Note to parents and teachers: Every effort has been made by the Publishers to ensure that these web sites are suitable for children, that they are of the highest educational value, and that they contain no inappropriate or offensive material. However, because of the nature of the Internet, it is impossible to guarantee that the contents of these sites will not be altered. We strongly advise that Internet access is supervised by a responsible adult.